Deacon Ilya Kokin

Sacred History from Adam to Me

Illustrations by Evgeny Podkolzin

Translated by Fr. John Hogg

Copyright © 2019 Exaltation Press

Author: Deacon Ilya Kokin
Illustrator: Evgeny Podkolzin
Translator: Fr. John Hogg

"Sacred History from Adam to Me"
      This book, by Deacon Ilya Kokin, is designed to teach children the basic overview of sacred history, starting with the Old and New Testaments and continuing with an overview of some of the persecutions that the Church has undergone, both ancient and modern, up to the present day.

All rights reserved. This book or any portion thereof may not be reproduced or used in any manner whatsoever without the express written permission of the publisher except for the use of brief quotations in a book review.

Translated from the original "Священная история от Адама до меня" by Nikea Press, Copyright © Trading house «NIKEA», www.Nikeabooks.ru

ISBN: 978-1-950067-09-1 (Paperback)

Edited by Cynthia Hogg

First printing edition 2019

Exaltation Press
Grand Rapids, MI

www.ExaltationPress.com

For bulk orders, please contact editor@exaltationpress.com.

Contents

THE MYSTERIOUS MASTER (INTRODUCTION)	9
ADAM LIVED IN A GARDEN OF PARADISE…	11
CRIME AND PUNISHMENT	16
REBOOTING HUMANITY	20
THE LORD GAVE AND THE LORD HAS TAKEN AWAY	26
ABRAHAM – THE FATHER OF THE FAITHFUL	28
UPWARDS!	32
ONE LIFE FOR THE WHOLE WORLD	34
WE'RE NOT SLAVES! YES, YOU ARE.	36
WHO ARE THE JUDGES?	42
THE BOY WHO LIVED	44
THE MAN WHO STOPPED THE RAIN	48
THE UNFULFILLED PROPHECY	51
I SEE HIM AFAR OFF…	52
THE THEOTOKOS	54
THE NATIVITY OF CHRIST	59
A LIFE-LONG ANTICIPATION	60
THE LAMB OF GOD	62
IN THE DESERT	64
HOW DO WE SEE GOD?	66
THROUGH THE ROOF	68
DEAD SOULS	70
JOY CONQUERS GRIEF	72
AN UNLEARNED LESSON	74
THE MYSTICAL SUPPER	76
AMBUSH	78
HOT AND COLD	80
THE CROSS	83
THE GRAVE	84
CHRIST IS RISEN!	86
A HEART ON FIRE	89
PEACE BE TO YOU	90
THE COMFORTER	92
THE LAST SHALL BE FIRST	94
FAITHFUL WITNESSES	98
PRINCE VLADIMIR'S SECRET	100
THE END AND A NEW BEGINNING	102
TODAY	104
THE HERO OF OUR TIME	107

THE MYSTERIOUS MASTER
(Introduction)

When I was little, I didn't yet believe in God but, like all children, in my heart, I wished He was real. At that time, it was easier for me to believe in fairy tales and one of them impressed me more than the others, a story called "The Little Red Flower." The part that fascinated me the most was when the girl, Anastasia, went off to live in an enchanted castle and there met the mysterious master of the castle.

Years later, when I was reading "The Little Red Flower" to my own child, I suddenly thought: mankind is a lot like the heroine of this story! I'm not referring to how we spend our whole childhood (and many spend a great deal longer) asking our parents for beautiful yet worthless things. Rather, I mean that we live in a world full of mystery and Someone, incredibly powerful and of limitless goodness, cares for us constantly, leaving little gifts for us here and there. But unfortunately, the Master of our world is unseen! We are afraid to meet Him and we picture Him as terrifying and scary but He isn't like that at all. We can discover what He's really like in only one way. We have to try to love Him. Only then will He be able to reveal Himself to us as He really is.

This book tells the story of how God spent centuries and millennia caring for mankind and how mankind learned to understand and love God.

Deacon Ilya Kokin

ADAM LIVED IN A GARDEN OF PARADISE...

Probably one of our most joyful childhood memories is Christmas morning, running to look under the tree to see what present is waiting for us, isn't it? Of course, all children understand that those presents don't appear by themselves just like the tree didn't grow by itself and the house didn't build itself. In the same way, this world that we have received as a gift did not come into being by itself. It was created by God, our wise and good Creator. Does that change anything for us? Of course! It changes everything! It means that our world is not a helpless speck of dust in a cold universe. Our world has meaning and purpose.

When He created our world, God worked toward His goal gradually. At first, water appeared and then fish, birds, and other animals... and what did God create everything out of? The Bible says "out of nothing." But not in the way that grown-ups mean it when

they don't want to answer a question. God is all-powerful and can do anything that He wants. Finally, human beings appeared — human beings who, unlike fish and birds, were able to understand and love their Creator! In order for us to be able to understand Him, we had to have something in common, some kind of "likeness." On the day he was born, Adam (for that was the name of the first human being) received from God many wonderful gifts — reason, free will, imagination, and even a wife with whom he immediately fell in love.

God knows all things and so He knew for certain what gifts would please Adam. (Being all-knowing is, after all, very useful when you're picking out a gift for someone.) And this young family was also given a nice place to live – a beautiful garden of Paradise. Everything was good, but...

...people always want what they don't have, don't they? God visited humanity in the garden and gave them a task. He told them to keep and cultivate this Paradise. Now the first part, keeping it, is easy to understand. That means that they needed to protect it and maintain good order. But what does it mean to "cultivate"? That means God entrusted humanity with the job of improving that which

He had created. The Creator trusted us to continue His work. The garden of Paradise was supposed to spread out over all the Earth. The whole Earth was supposed to become Paradise. Paradise had borders. Human freedom also had limits. The Lord forbade people under fear of death to eat from one of the trees in Paradise, the Tree of the Knowledge of Good and Evil. And so, that was the gift they wanted – fruit from the forbidden tree! But what kind of strange tree was this? How can you learn good and evil by biting into a piece of fruit? It sounds a bit like the mushroom from the story "Alice in Wonderland": you grow if you eat from one side of it and shrink if you eat from the other side. So, was the tree something like that? One wise person explained it this way: having tasted the fruit, humanity discovered that obedience to God is good and that disobedience is evil. They were deceived by the ancient serpent, the Devil (an angel who was unfaithful to God and became

His enemy) and thought that by doing what was forbidden, they would be as free and as all-powerful as God. But that isn't how things work. When we follow someone's advice, we become like that person. When they obeyed the Devil instead of God, the first human beings became like him and damaged the "divine likeness" in themselves – they no longer understood or loved their Creator. It became harder for people to love at all and so they began to fight with each other. And there was no longer a place for them in the garden of Paradise. Of course, they were very upset but God comforted them, telling them, "Someday Someone will be born Who will fix everything and will restore Paradise to humanity."

CRIME AND PUNISHMENT

Stories really come alive when someone commits a crime. A clever villain commits a mysterious murder and covers his tracks but then a shrewd detective appears and brings it all to light. Why do we love detective stories so much? It's not so much the mystery and the chase we love as much as the fact that in detective stories, justice always triumphs and the villain gets what he deserves. That's what happens in books but in real life, things often don't work out that way. Does that mean that in ordinary life, many criminals go unpunished? Not at all. Crime never goes unpunished. We can see

that in the story of the very first murder. Adam and Eve had sons who were named Cain and Abel. Each of them did what he liked best. Cain was a farmer while Abel tended herds of animals. After the disobedience of Adam and Eve, human beings didn't lose their free will entirely. And God still cared for them. But something had changed. Before, God was the only one who gave gifts. Now, to try to make up for their sins against Him, humanity started to bring gifts to God, called "sacrifices." Each person offered to the Lord what he had. A farmer would offer Him the fruits of the Earth and a herdsman would offer some of his animals.

Once, when the brothers brought their offerings to God, the Lord rejected Cain's offering because it was insincere. God wanted Cain to realize that, but an evil man never looks for the cause of his misfortunes

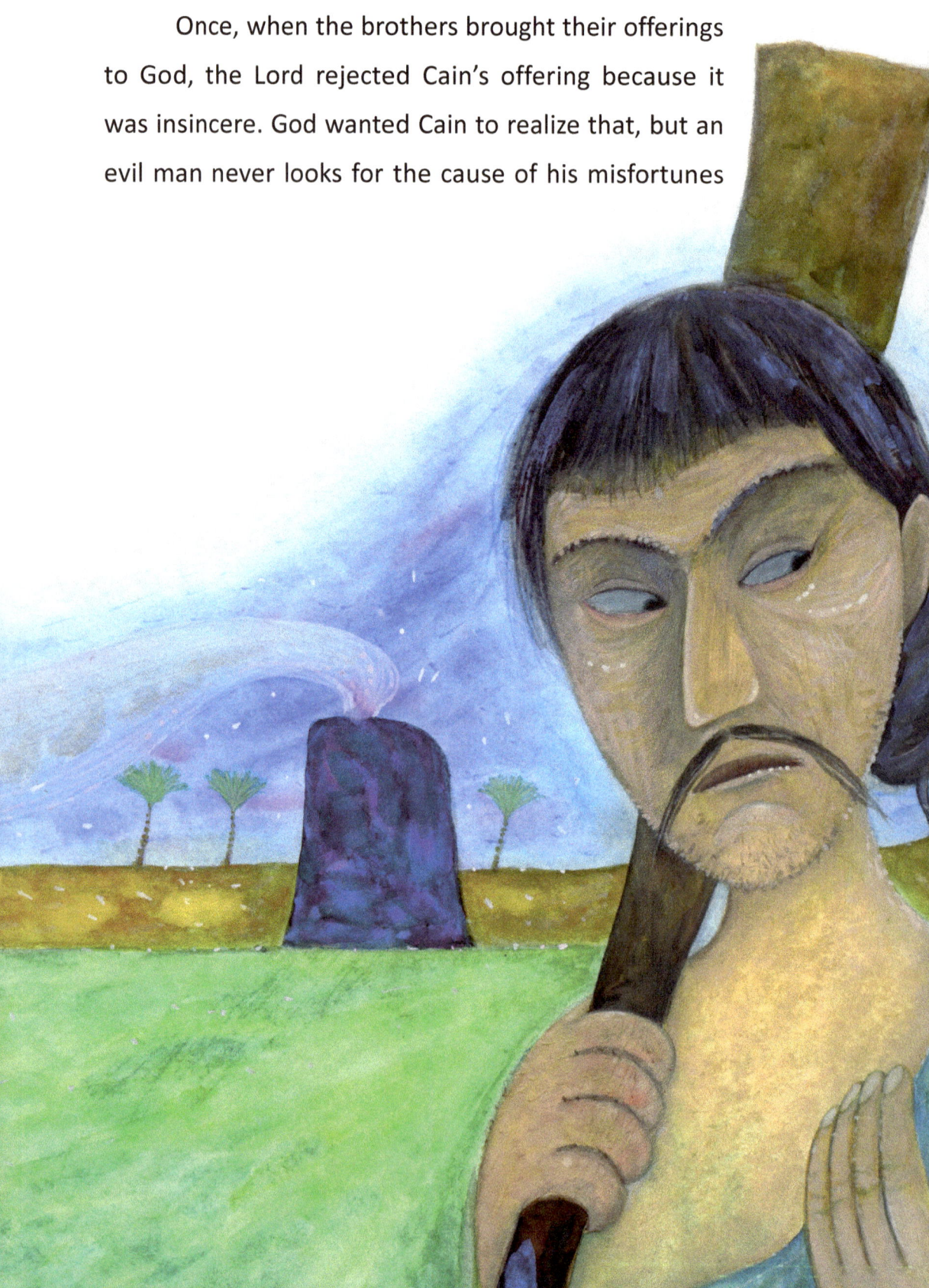

in himself. He always blames others. And Cain found someone to blame (not that there were many people to choose from then). He blamed his younger brother, Abel. Cain led his brother into a field and killed him. In those days, there were no detectives, no judges, and no prisons. The Lord God Himself judged the murderer. The Bible talks about some kind of mysterious "mark" or "sign" that was placed on Cain from then on. What was it? It's hard to say but one thing is clear: evil always changes a person from the inside and other people can see that. And isn't that the worst punishment of all?

REBOOTING HUMANITY

You've probably never heard the word "antediluvian," have you? It's a long word. But what does it mean? Literally, it means "before the flood." But what flood was so important that it got its own word? That we can learn from the Bible. After the story of Cain and Abel, several centuries passed and the descendants of Adam and Eve spread out throughout the world. Whole cities appeared. And then all of that came to an end and civilization disappeared from the face of the Earth. However, this didn't happen suddenly. One man knew about the impending disaster in advance and even tried to warn everyone else but no one wanted to listen to him. That man was

called Noah.

People laughed at Noah and thought he was eccentric but the truth was the opposite. Noah was the only one who knew the terrible truth about the coming flood because he was the only one who listened to and obeyed God. Everyone else preferred knowing nothing about God. That was why, for the first and only time in history, the Lord made a terrifying decision. He decided to send a great flood on the Earth to cleanse evil and violence from the face of the Earth and start everything from scratch. God told righteous Noah to make a large boat, an ark, and gather all of the animals into

it, two of each kind, so that after the flood, life could be reborn.

    A lot depends on how you choose to look at something. You could look at the flood as the destruction of humanity but the truth is that the flood was the beginning of humanity's rebirth. Although Noah seemed insignificant, through him everything ended well. When the flood was over, Noah and the other passengers of the ark gave thanks to God for His mercy and in response, they saw His rainbow in the sky.

THE LORD GAVE AND THE LORD HAS TAKEN AWAY

The waters of the flood receded and the time came to ask an important question. How is it that human beings whom God has created to be good can turn evil? We remember from the story of the first human beings that the Devil (a fallen angel who fights against God and mankind) turned humanity towards the path of evil. But how exactly does that happen? Christians call it "temptation." To turn good people into bad people, the Devil tempts them. Temptation is an unseen war. The Bible shows us the secrets of how that war works. The story of Job the Much-suffering is a clear example of this.

Job was "the greatest of all the sons of the East." He was renowned as much for his riches as for his piety, a rare combination. The Bible recounts a remarkable conversation that took place between God and the Devil.

"Well, of course Job brings You sacrifices," the Devil taunted, "because he's as rich as a king. Let's see what tune he'll be singing if You take away his riches and good health!"

"Okay," the Lord answered. "We will see. His riches and his body are in your power, only leave his soul alone."

That very day, Job lost his houses and cattle. He also lost something much more valuable – his children – and his body was covered with sores. "The Lord gave and the Lord has taken away," was how the righteous man humbly responded, "blessed be the name of the Lord!" The Devil had lost and so the Lord gave Job back his health, his riches, his good name, and the joy of fatherhood.

So what exactly is "temptation"? Despite what we often think, "temptation" doesn't really mean a trap or some kind of force that makes us do something. Temptation is a test. And look at what the Lord does when He allows Job to be tempted. God allows the Devil to take his life apart like the layers of a Russian nesting doll, layer by layer. Job loses his riches, his children, and his health all so that he can see what his true riches have always been – his immortal soul. God doesn't allow the Devil to touch Job's soul. Only we can harm our own souls by allowing evil into our hearts and cooperating with it.

ABRAHAM – THE FATHER OF THE FAITHFUL

Biblical history is built around the lives of God's chosen. But being "chosen" doesn't mean that someone is God's favorite. God, like a wise father, loves all of His children equally. But His chosen are those who answered God's love by loving Him in return. This is the story of another such chosen person whom the Bible calls the "father of the faithful." His name is Abraham.

Sometimes the Lord sets His chosen ones apart from other

people, each in a particular way. Adam lived by himself in the garden of Paradise, Noah alone listened to God and was saved in the ark, and Job bore poverty and sickness and the loneliness that comes with them. Likewise, God separated Abraham from his people. God worked with Abraham like a gardener who carefully transplants a valuable plant from wild surroundings into a greenhouse in order to care for it. The Lord told this righteous man to leave behind his home country and go where He showed him. Abraham did as he was told and left everything behind and went to a foreign country, into the unknown. That was the first time, but certainly not the last, that Abraham showed his deep faith in the Lord. However, believing in God doesn't mean blind submission. The Bible tells us about one occasion when Abraham showed great stubbornness when talking with God.

Once the Lord revealed to His servant Abraham that He was going to punish two nearby cities where evil reigned. When

Abraham heard it, he objected, saying, "Are there really no righteous people there? Not even fifty?" God answered that if there were fifty righteous people there, He would have mercy on the two cities. "And if there are only twenty?" Abraham asked. "I will have mercy for the sake of twenty," the Lord answered. "And if is is just ten?" Abraham continued (for people from the East are good at bargaining!) The Lord agreed to have mercy on the cities even if only ten righteous people could be found. This story shows us what the Lord's words mean when He says, "I desire mercy and not a sacrifice."

These words of the Lord were also demonstrated by another occurrence. God promised Abraham, His chosen one, that he would have a multitude of

descendants. Abraham waited and hoped. He was already old when at long last, his son Isaac was born. The new father loved his son very much but then his faith was put to a new test, the most difficult one he would face in his life. God told Abraham to offer as a sacrifice... his own son. Abraham's heart bled for his son. He would rather give his own life instead. This time, however, Abraham did not bargain. But right before he could deliver the fatal knife blow, God stopped Abraham's hand. What happened wasn't just a cruel whim on God's part. The Lord wanted to show us what true sacrifice is: when you're ready to part with someone that you love more than your own life. Several centuries later, God Himself offered His Son as a sacrifice. For whom? For us!

UPWARDS!

When the first created man sinned, he lost Paradise and an angel with a flaming sword in its hand began to guard the way back into Paradise – that is what the Bible tells us. Perhaps, however, the angel standing at the entrance isn't just there to stop us from entering. Perhaps, on the contrary, it is there to show us where the entrance is. After all, there is fire in its hand, fire that can be seen day and night. Sometimes, that entrance to Paradise is revealed to holy people like it was to righteous Jacob, the grandson of Abraham. Once, while he was sleeping, Jacob had a vision of a ladder going from Earth to Heaven, with angels traveling on it. It is difficult to say how many steps the ladder that leads to Heaven has but one thing is clear: every time we overcome some evil in our hearts and learn to do good, we take another step, moving upwards to Heaven.

ONE LIFE FOR THE WHOLE WORLD

But we don't only become better when we we choose between good and evil and prefer what is good. We grow a little closer to God even when we choose the lesser of two evils. The story of righteous Joseph, the son of Jacob, the great-grandson of Abraham, is an example of this. This story shows us how feeling pity for one person saved an entire people. That people even has a very wise saying: "Whoever saves a single life saves the whole world."

Many people know how difficult it can be to get along

with older siblings. Righteous Joseph had ten brothers who were older than him! And parents often give more attention to younger children than to older ones. At least, that's how it was with Joseph. Once, his father gave him some fine clothing. A small thing, right? But remember that from the time of Cain and Abel on, envy has led people to commit murder. Here as well, Joseph's brothers agreed to kill their "father's favorite" and pass it all off as an accident. But one of them, Judah, had pity on Joseph and convinced the others not to kill him but just to sell him into slavery to some passing merchants. Many years later, when Joseph had gone from being a slave to being the Egyptian Pharaoh's most trusted counselor, he was able to save his whole family from dying of hunger.

WE'RE NOT SLAVES! YES, YOU ARE.

Joseph brought his family from Palestine, where there was a famine, to the land of plenty, Egypt. Centuries passed and the twelves sons of Jacob (another son was born after Joseph) became the forefathers of God's chosen people, the Jews. They were the twelve patriarchs. The word "patriarch" means "forefather."

The Egyptians were very unhappy that the descendants of Jacob

had settled in their country. "Egypt for Egyptians!" they said. They began to oppress the Jews until they had no rights and were basically slaves. Then, the Lord sent the Jews another of His chosen ones, named Moses. If Jacob saved his people from hunger, Moses was the one who saved them from slavery, giving them back their freedom and their own country.

God spoke to His chosen servant from a flaming bush (surprisingly, the bush burned yet was not consumed). It was truly a remarkable conversation! God knew Moses even when he was still in his mother's womb and so He addressed him by name. But Moses did not know Who was speaking with him and so he asked the Stranger to introduce Himself and tell him His name. And here, just like Moses, we learn God's name as "Yahweh," which means "the Ever-living." That's who God is. He is Life itself! God commanded the prophet to go to the Egyptian Pharaoh and ask that he free the Jewish people.

"What if Pharaoh doesn't listen to me?" asked Moses.

"Do not be afraid," God answered, "I will be with you. You will work many wondrous miracles. But first, you should practice. Throw your staff on the ground."

Moses threw his staff and turned pale. The staff had turned into a snake! Think of Adam. He was deceived by a snake and lost eternal life. However, when someone obeys the voice of God, they can even take a snake by the tail without fear because it won't be able to harm them.

Miracles accompanied Moses both when he tried to convince

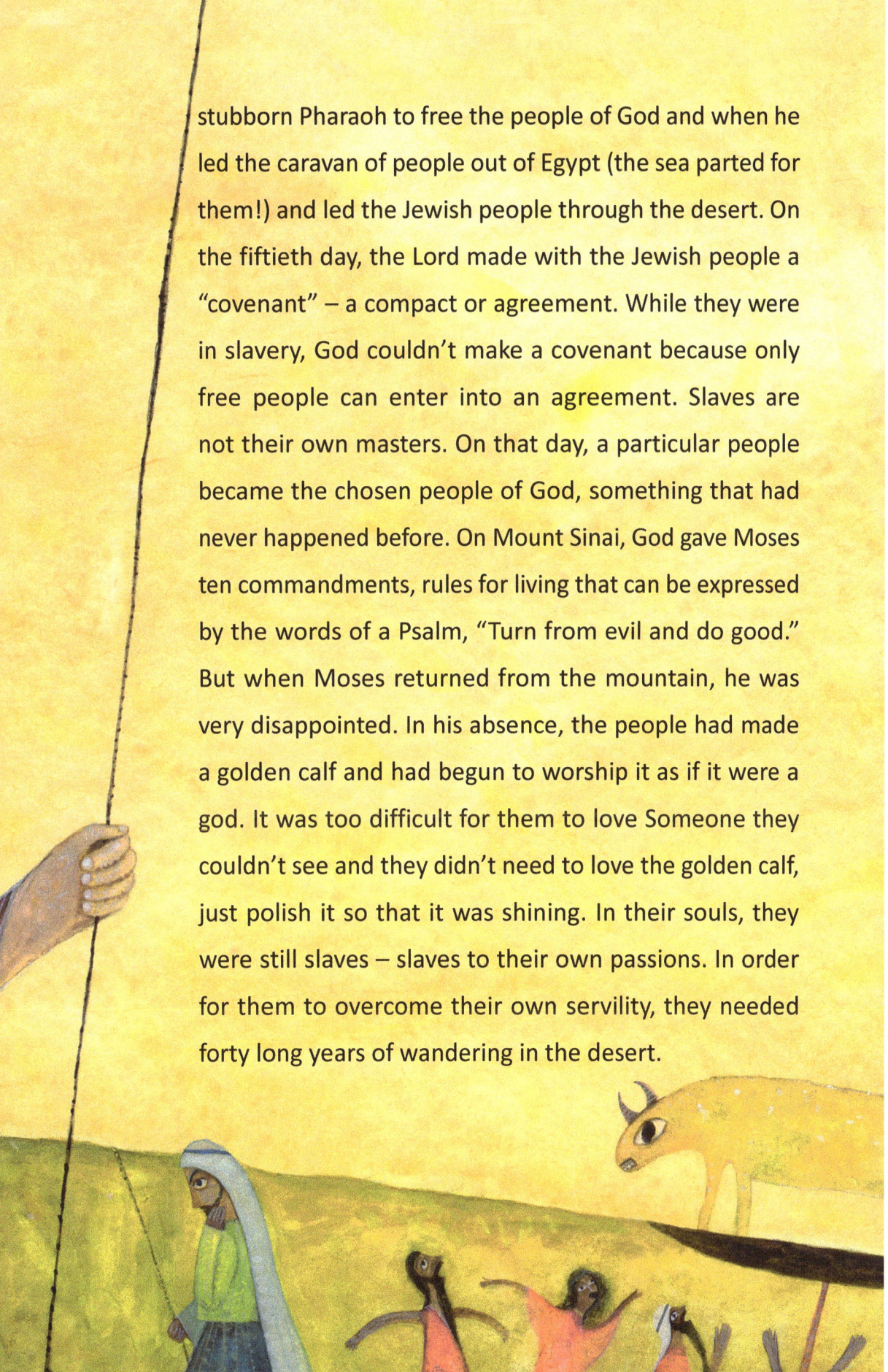

stubborn Pharaoh to free the people of God and when he led the caravan of people out of Egypt (the sea parted for them!) and led the Jewish people through the desert. On the fiftieth day, the Lord made with the Jewish people a "covenant" – a compact or agreement. While they were in slavery, God couldn't make a covenant because only free people can enter into an agreement. Slaves are not their own masters. On that day, a particular people became the chosen people of God, something that had never happened before. On Mount Sinai, God gave Moses ten commandments, rules for living that can be expressed by the words of a Psalm, "Turn from evil and do good." But when Moses returned from the mountain, he was very disappointed. In his absence, the people had made a golden calf and had begun to worship it as if it were a god. It was too difficult for them to love Someone they couldn't see and they didn't need to love the golden calf, just polish it so that it was shining. In their souls, they were still slaves – slaves to their own passions. In order for them to overcome their own servility, they needed forty long years of wandering in the desert.

WHO ARE THE JUDGES?

Over the course of history, God's chosen ones matured and became more responsible. Adam was unable to bear the responsibility of caring for the garden of Paradise and its inhabitants and couldn't even answer for his own wife before God. Noah, however, handled his task very well. He cared both for his family and for the animals that were saved from the flood in the ark. And then Abraham and Moses had to answer for the fate of an entire people! Now we are going to talk about one of God's chosen servants who did something even greater. He saved the entire Jewish people by sacrificing... well, let's start at the beginning. The Prophet Moses had led the Jewish people to Palestine, the Promised Land.

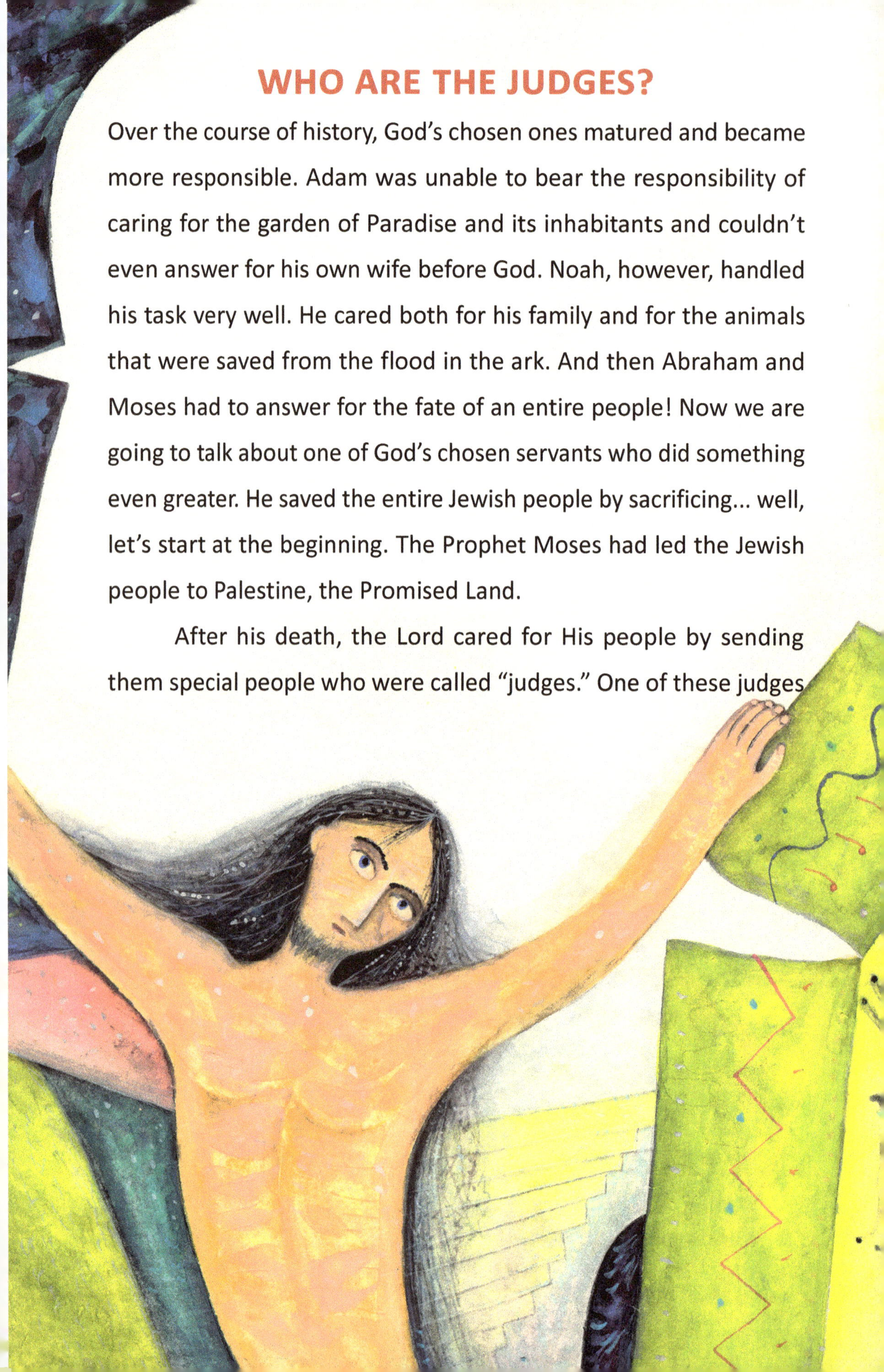

After his death, the Lord cared for His people by sending them special people who were called "judges." One of these judges

was a mighty man named Samson. If he had lived in the Middle Ages, he would have been the sort of knight that songs and legends are written about. He worked many mighty deeds. This continued until his enemies found out how to defeat this mighty man. As a sign of his special service to God, Samson had made a vow never to cut his hair. As long as he kept his vow, God made him stronger than any other human being. However, once Samson told his secret to his friend and she told his enemies all about it. While Samson was sleeping the deep sleep of a mighty man, they cut his hair, tied him up, and blinded him. A little while later, his enemies brought him tied up like a wild beast to a feast where all of their nobles were gathered. By that time, Samson's hair had grown out again and his strength had returned. At the festival, Samson did his last mighty work. He knocked over the arches supporting the hall, taking his enemies with him. Samson was the first to save the Jewish people by sacrificing his own life.

The Boy Who Lived

When a mighty warrior like Samson heroically does battle against an enemy, it's exciting but it doesn't seem like a miracle. But when instead of a warrior, a young boy comes out to do battle, that couldn't be anything other than a miracle! That, too, happened in the Bible. Once, an enemy made war on the Israelites (another name for the people of God). A gigantic, fierce warrior named Goliath came out to meet the Jewish people. He began to laugh at the Jews and their God. He mocked them and made fun of them and asked if there was any brave man among them who would come out and fight him in single combat. No one dared. Just then, a young shepherd boy named David came to visit his older brothers. He was still just a little boy who had never seen battle before, but Goliath's impudence made him so angry that he decided to take up Goliath's challenge and fight him. The leader of the Jewish army gave the brave boy his armor and weapons but the chain mail was too big for him and so David set out for the duel in his ordinary clothing.

For his weapon, he chose some stones and a sling, a piece of cloth shepherds used for throwing things to chase wild dogs away from their flocks. When Goliath saw that a child had come to fight him, he was offended – but not for long. One quick shot right on target and Goliath fell down dead. David defeated his enemy with an ordinary sling.

But how do we defeat our enemies? We also have a powerful weapon – the words "I forgive you." Our enemies don't expect that from us. When they hear the words "I forgive you," our enemies stumble in surprise and some of them even become friends.

THE WISE KING

After a while, David became king in Israel. He ruled long and happily because his favorite thing to do wasn't throwing banquets or hunting, but praying. He composed many wonderful hymns, the Psalms. Even today, when we turn to God in prayer, we usually use the words of King David. God promised his chosen servant David that the Christ, the Savior of the world, would be his descendant. After David died, his son Solomon sat on his throne. During his reign, the first temple of God was built in Jerusalem. Solomon became king when he was still very young and so he asked God to give him the wisdom to rule God's chosen people. God gave him what he asked for because God is never stingy in giving good things. Solomon, however, never forgot to Whom he owed his wisdom. "Hope on the Lord with all your heart and do not depend on your on your own reasoning," he said.

THE MAN WHO STOPPED THE RAIN

Not all the kings of Israel were holy. Far from it. Some of them forgot the Lord and preferred the "gods" that neighboring people worshiped. Pagan gods are simple and predictable while the God of Israel was too mysterious and difficult to understand. In order to please Him, you had to keep His commandments – don't kill, don't steal, be faithful... They weren't even allowed to envy! But all the pagan "gods" needed to be happy was a sacrifice. At least, that's what their priests said. It's like in school. If you want to understand something, really to learn it, you have to read, think, do

your homework... But if you're okay getting a C, you can just copy someone else's answers.

So whenever the Jews forgot their God and began to look to their neighbors' "gods," the Lord sent them prophets. A prophet is a holy person who tells people what the will of God is. One of the brightest prophets in the Bible was St. Elijah. When Israel had once again forgotten about God, the prophet Elijah appeared. At first, he tried to convince the people by kind words but when that didn't work, he had to try harsher measures. "From now on there will be neither rain nor dew until I say!" Then there was a drought in the land that lasted for three and a half years. Afterwards, the prophet went to see the king and demanded that he call together the whole people. When they had all gathered, Elijah turned to the pagan priests and said, "Let's build two altars and put our sacrifices on them and pray. I will pray to my God and you will pray to yours. And whichever one accepts the sacrifice by burning it with fire, that is the true God." Everyone liked the idea except for the pagan priests but they couldn't get out of it. All day, they tried casting spells but nothing happened. "Pray louder," Elijah mocked. "Maybe your god is asleep?" Finally, Elijah himself began to pray and fire came down from Heaven and burned up the sacrifice he had prepared. What amazing power God gives His saints!

THE UNFULFILLED PROPHECY

Besides revealing God's will to people and working miracles, the prophets often foretold the future. However, the Bible tells the story of one prophecy that went unfulfilled. That is the story of the Prophet Jonah whom the Lord sent to the city of Nineveh. Nineveh's inhabitants had forgotten the difference between good and evil, so they did more evil than good. Jonah didn't want to go and tried to hide. But how can you hide from God who sees everything? Even on the bottom of the ocean, He will find us. Eventually, though, Jonah did go to Nineveh and began to frighten the inhabitants of the city: "In forty days, this city will be destroyed because of your sins!" And a miracle happened – they believed him! The whole city, from the king to the beggars, began to repent of their sins and ask God for forgiveness. And of course, the merciful Lord forgave them. Then, Jonah began to be upset: "What kind of a prophet am I if my prophecy isn't fulfilled?" he lamented, sitting near the city that had been saved. It was very hot out and so the prophet was sitting in the shade of a plant. Suddenly, right before Jonah's very eyes, the plant dried up and its dead leaves fell to the ground. "Are you upset?" the Lord asked Jonah. "Very!" the prophet answered, almost in tears. "You see? You have pity on the plant," God said to him, "and yet you're surprised that I had mercy on a whole city!"

I SEE HIM AFAR OFF...

Most of the time, prophets foretold events that would come to pass soon. Usually, like in the story of Jonah, it was necessary to help the people understand. But the Bible also contains a series of prophecies that did not come to pass right away. These are the prophecies which told about the life of the Savior of the world, the incarnate Son of God. The Lord Himself first told Adam and Eve about the coming birth of the Christ, saying, "The child born of the Woman will crush the serpent's head." The Prophet Isaiah calls that mysterious Woman a "Virgin." And the Prophet Micah predicted the exact birthplace of the Savior, the city of Bethlehem. The Prophet Zachariah described the Lord's triumphant entrance into Jerusalem and how He would then be betrayed for thirty pieces of silver. The same Prophet Isaiah predicted the Christ's voluntary sacrifice for the sins of the world: "He took on our infirmities and bore our diseases. By His wounds we have been healed." And the prophet Hosea predicted the resurrection of Christ, "at the dawning of the third day."

THE THEOTOKOS

If God had already given the promise of His Son's birth to Adam and Eve, why did so much time (thousands of years!) pass before the Savior was born? Because the Woman who could become Christ's Mother still hadn't arrived. The Lord, like a wise and patient gardener, first planted a seed and then watered and cared for it, getting rid of the weeds that could choke out the delicate little plant. And when the tree had grown, the Lord pruned from it the dry branches that didn't bear fruit. All of this He did with one goal in mind. He wanted a special Flower to blossom on the tree – the Theotokos. That Flower, in turn, would bring forth fruit at the appointed time, Christ the Savior. The Mother of God was born in the family of an elderly couple, Joachim and Anna, who had given up hope of ever being parents. God often works that way. He begins to act when we no longer trust in our own strength. It's like in a conversation. While one person is talking, the other has to be quiet, even if he has something to say. Joachim and Anna gave their daughter the name Mary which means "Lady." The fate of all of humanity depended on this special Lady.

When a young couple has a child, they often dote on their newborn baby. Joachim and Anna,

however, were already old and they understood that God had given them a Daughter not just for themselves. The Lord had need of Her. And so, when she turned three years old, they took Mary to be raised in the Temple of God, where she spent about ten years praying, reading the Scriptures, and working with her hands. Then, Mary's education in the Temple came to an end and she went back

to the city where she was born, to Nazareth. Once, as Mary was reading the Bible – the prophecy of Isaiah about the miraculous Virgin who would give birth to Christ – an Angel appeared to Her and said, "Rejoice! Those words are speaking of you. You are that Virgin." Could any news be more joyful? The Virgin Mary answered the Angel, "I am the handmaiden of the Lord. Let it be to me according to your word."

THE NATIVITY OF CHRIST

The Bible is a surprising book. Sometimes it might seem like it was written about people who lived a long time ago in a galaxy far, far away. But really, the Bible was written for and about us. Does that mean that the prophecy of Isaiah is for us, too? Of course! Christ Himself says so when He says, "Whoever fulfills the Will of God will be like My Mother." When we obey God's commandments, God works through us, through our hands, through our words. He is incarnate over and over again through us. However, His birth from the Virgin Mary is, of course, unique and unrepeatable. Not long before giving birth, the Theotokos set out on a journey to Bethlehem with her protector, the righteous Joseph. For it was in Bethlehem, according to a Biblical prophecy, that the Savior would be born. The Holy Family went from house to house but no one would give them a place to spend the night. Even if the inhabitants of Bethlehem remembered the ancient prophecy, they never imagined that it was speaking about them and their time. They never expected to see the Mother of the Savior at the their own doorsteps. And so, the Holy Family settled in for the night in a cave where shepherds sometimes left their flocks. Unlike us, the animals were always ready to meet God and so they were the ones that became witnesses of His miraculous Nativity.

A LIFE-LONG ANTICIPATION

It wasn't only the sheep, rabbits, and donkeys who saw the newborn Divine Child. In those days in Israel, there were also holy people who were found worthy of the mystery of Christ's Nativity. Some of them lived near Bethlehem, some had to travel a great distance, and one lived an incredibly long life in order to see the Savior.

The first of these were the shepherds who heard the good news of the birth of Christ from the Angels. The second were the

wise men who studied the stars and came from the distant land of Persia to worship the Savior. The shepherds who believed the Angels symbolize the path of faith. The wise men, who studied the stars, who acted "according to science" symbolize the path of reason. The path of faith is shorter but either path, if followed to the end, leads to Christ. The Bible tells us about another man who in the course of his life joined together the way of faith and of knowledge. That man was named Simeon. By the time of Christ's birth, he was about three hundred years old. This was the secret of his long life: when he was younger, he was a scholar who took part in translating the Bible into Greek. He was given the passage from the Prophet Isaiah to translate that talked about the Theotokos being a virgin. Simeon thought that there must be some mistake in the text but at that minute, an Angel appeared to him and said, "That prophecy is the truth and if you do not believe, you will see it with your own eyes!" Simeon began to wait. Years passed, then decades and centuries but Simeon waited and had faith. Finally, the Lord revealed to him that his waiting had come to an end: the very same Virgin and Child which the prophecy spoke about are coming to the Temple today. Hurry to go meet them!

THE LAMB OF GOD

When the Lord Jesus Christ had just been born, only a few people learned of His birth but when He grew up and became a grown Man, the whole world learned of Him. In those days, on the banks of the river Jordan, not far from Nazareth, the prophet John was preaching. He spoke about simple things that were easy to understand: "If you have extra clothing, give it to the poor. If you have an extra piece of bread, give it to someone who is hungry. Do not hurt or deceive anyone." It sounds so easy! But for some reason, those simple things are the hardest to follow. It is as if there were a voice in our soul, turning us away from doing what is right, "You don't have to do that. Others people will take care of it. Or you can do it later. And if you don't do it ever, nothing bad will happen…" We call that voice "sin." As a sign of repentance, a sign of the cleansing of the soul from everything that is evil and sinful, John washed those who came to him in the waters of the river Jordan. "I wash you with water," he said,

"but soon Someone is coming who will deliver you from the power of sin."

Finally, that day arrived. John noticed the Savior coming to him from a long way off. He turned to the crowd that had gathered and pointed to the Man in the distance and said joyfully, "Behold the Lamb of God!" When Christ drew near, everyone held their breath and waited to see what would happen. To their surprise, He asked John to wash Him in the river, just like all the others. "But why?" John objected, "I am not worthy to untie Your sandals." "It must happen," the Lord answered. It is always surprising when someone who can do whatever they want does what is necessary and right.

IN THE DESERT

How can we be delivered from the power of sin? Only by fighting against it and conquering it. And where is the best place to fight against sin? Where it lives. God is Life and so when we look at everything that is alive – the delicate flowers, the lovely fish, the singing birds – we cannot help wanting to praise Him. But sin is death and so we can best confront it in the lifeless desert. That was where the Savior went when He went out of the river Jordan. For forty days, He prayed and fasted, not eating

anything, and on the fortieth day, the Devil, appeared to Him, the Devil who as a serpent had tempted Adam and Eve and infected them with the poison of sin. And the fight began. "Are you hungry?" the serpent asked with false concern. "Eat! After all, it would be easy for you to turn one of these stones into bread." "The Word of God is more important than bread," the Lord answered. "Oh, You know the Word of God?" the Devil asked, changing tactics and instantly transporting the Savior to the roof of the temple. "What does it say in the Scriptures? His Angels will bear you in their arms so that you will not strike your foot against a stone...?" The evil one smiled and pointed down. "The Scriptures say that you shall not tempt the Lord your God," was Christ's answer. "Okay then," the Devil responded, "in that case, I will give You all the riches and glory of this world if you just worship me. I won't tell anyone." The Savior responded "Only God alone should be worshiped." Christ is called the New Adam because He also became the first man – the first Man who did not submit to the Devil.

HOW DO WE SEE GOD?

God is invisible and so He can be hard to get to know and hard to love since you cannot love Someone you don't know. However, the Savior taught us how we can see God who is invisible. To see God, we must cleanse our hearts from evil and then we will see God, not with our physical eyes, but with our heart. Christ also taught us how to love God: by doing what is just and honorable and not lying or deceiving others. Most important of all, we should always help our neighbor. And who is our neighbor? It isn't complicated. Our neighbors are the people nearby, the people all around us.

Also, in order to love God, we have to pray to Him, to talk with Him. But what can we talk with God about? Well, what do we talk to our neighbors about? We ask them about themselves, or tell them about what is going on with us, or thank them for something, or ask them for something. In the same way, we can thank God, ask Him questions, tell Him about what is going on with us, or ask Him for our needs. God is our kind Father and if we ask Him for bread, He will never give us "a stone or a scorpion" instead. The problem is we often ask Him for the wrong things. Instead of asking Him for bread, we might ask Him for a stone (something useless) or even a scorpion (something that would be dangerous for us). The best thing that we can ask God for is His help in cleansing our hearts from evil and to forgive us our sins. In order to do that, however, we ourselves have to learn to forgive.

THROUGH THE ROOF

Wherever He went, Jesus Christ was followed by a crowd of people. He often talked with them, telling them about the mysteries of the Kingdom of Heaven and how to become a citizen of that Kingdom. The Savior spoke with authority, unlike everyone who had come before Him. Everyone understood that He knew what He was talking about. Only the King Himself – God incarnate – could talk that way about the Kingdom of Heaven. After a while, Christ chose out of His followers

twelve disciples who became the Apostles.

However, people did not only follow Christ to listen to Him speak. Many followed Him hoping to be healed of their diseases or to witness a miracle. Tales of His miracles were spreading throughout the Near East: "They say He fed five thousand people with five loaves of bread." "I saw Him heal a blind man." "My brother saw Him raise the dead!" Once, Christ was talking with the people in a house that was overcrowded when four people came, carrying their friend on a stretcher. He was very ill and unable to walk. Because of the crowd, they couldn't squeeze into the house and so they took off part of the roof and lowered the stretcher down right in front of Christ's feet. That makes sense: in order to meet our Heavenly King, we have to take off the roof of our earthly dwelling, whether that "roof" is our delusions, prejudices or passions. That day, the sick man was healed both in body and soul since the Lord also forgave him his sins.

DEAD SOULS

The Lord said that healing the soul from sin is more important than healing the body from illness because our mortal body is temporary but our soul is eternal and He revealed an important secret to us: If we don't want our souls to be overcome by a spiritual disease, we need to begin treatment at the first symptoms. Theft begins with envy, murder begins with anger, and betrayal begins with indifference. It is very important to learn to pull sin out from our

soul while the sin is still like a little seedling because it is much harder to uproot a fully grown tree.

Just like for our bodies, the main condition for the treatment of our souls is admitting what the problem is: I am sick and I need treatment. The most difficult cases are when people are seriously ill but think they are healthy. In the time of Christ, there were people who thought they were righteous. They were called the Pharisees. They thought the most important thing was not to commit sins in their actions but they failed to see what was going on in their hearts. Christ called them hypocrites. The Lord accused the Pharisees, saying, "When you wash a dish, you wash it inside and out. Why then do you only care about the purity of your body and not about the purity of your soul?"

JOY CONQUERS GRIEF

By the power of His words and even more by His miraculous deeds, the Lord Jesus convinced His disciples that He is the Son of God. But there is one particular miracle the Savior did, His most well known one, that shows us not only His divinity but also His humanity. One of Jesus's friends died. His name was Lazarus. In those days, there were no trains or planes and so the Lord only arrived at the village where Lazarus had lived four days after he had been buried. Everyone was horrified when Christ told them to open the tomb but then... He raised His friend from the dead! There is one especially moving detail in this story. Even though

He knew in advance that Lazarus would soon be alive and well, as a human being, Jesus wept as He stood before the sealed tomb of His friend.

This all took place not far from Jerusalem and so all the inhabitants of the capital city learned about the miracle that had taken place that same day. And when Christ entered Jerusalem the next day, they greeted Him like a King returning victorious from battle. And so it was – the day before, the Savior had won a great victory against our most feared enemy, death! Christ rode on a donkey and people spread out in front of him their robes and palm branches. Everyone, from the small to the great, cried out, "Blessed is the King of Israel!" Only the Pharisees didn't join in the general celebration because they hated Christ from the beginning. As the triumphant procession approached the city gates, the Savior again shed tears. He looked at Jerusalem and whispered, "Jerusalem, Jerusalem! How often I wanted to gather your children up like a hen gathers her chicks under her wings but you would not! Today as well, you do not really recognize me..."

AN UNLEARNED LESSON

What did Christ mean by these sorrowful words? The Lord knew that in a few days the same people who followed Him and greeted Him with songs of praise would cry out without pity for Him to be crucified. The days of the Jewish Passover were approaching. Passover was when they celebrated the deliverance of the Jewish people from slavery to the Egyptians. More than a thousand years had passed since then, yet they had not learned their lesson and so history was repeating itself. When faced with a choice between God

and a golden calf, the people of God once again chose the calf of slavery, but this time Roman rather than Egyptian.

For Israel, faithfulness to an earthly king, the Roman Emperor, proved more important than their loyalty to the King of Heaven. Christ knew all this and suffered at their unfaithfulness. However, we all know that no betrayal can wound us as deeply as that of a close friend. There was one such person in Christ's inner circle. Judas, one of the twelve Apostles, was planning on betraying His Teacher. Not just betraying, but selling Him out. He appeared before the chief priests and offered to give them Christ when He would be alone. For his betrayal, they paid him a measly thirty silver coins.

THE MYSTICAL SUPPER

Only a few hours were left until His betrayal but only Judas and Christ Himself were aware of that. The Apostles, not suspecting anything, prepared supper to celebrate Passover with their Teacher. This farewell supper has come to be known as the "Mystical Supper." Today, when we enter a house, we might wash our hands but in those days, they also washed their feet, since they walked around hot and dusty roads with only sandals on their feet. Usually, it was the servants who washed the feet of people who had just arrived but Christ and His Apostles were poor people and had no servants. Nevertheless, none of the Apostles expected Christ to do what He did next. He took a pitcher and washed the disciples feet Himself. "I came into this world to serve mankind, not to be served," Christ said to explain His strange action. Supper began. Everyone felt that something was wrong. "One of you will betray

me." Christ's quiet words hit them like thunder from a clear blue sky.

They all looked at each other. How would normal people have behaved if they were in the Apostles' places? They would have begun to suspect each other ("Because it obviously cannot be me!") But Christ's disciples were very special (well, all of them except one). After having spent years with the Lord, they had learned something important. They had learned to take responsibility on themselves. Each of them, then, began to ask, "Is it I?" "What do you think?" Jesus answered each of them, quietly. But that wasn't the only strange thing about this supper. During the Passover meal, the people usually ate a lamb in memory of the lamb whose blood Moses had smeared on their doors to keep them from death. At the end of the supper, the Savior took bread and divided it among His disciples, saying, "This is My Body." Then, He took a cup of wine and said, "This is My Blood of the New Testament which is shed for the forgiveness of sins." This is what John the Baptist had been talking about when He called the Savior "the Lamb of God." Today, when we approach the Chalice at Liturgy, we enter into the New Covenant with God. This new covenant is not just with one people but with all of humanity.

AMBUSH

After supper, late in the evening, Christ set out with His disciples for the garden of Gethsemane to pray. This is where Judas had planned an ambush for the Teacher. However, this wasn't a surprise for Christ. "All of you will abandon me today," He said to His Apostles on the road. The Apostles all began to object. Peter, one of the disciples who was closest to Christ, began to argue the loudest. "What do You mean?" he said. "I am ready to die for You!" "To die for Me?" Christ repeated, looking at Peter with a sad smile. "Today you will deny Me three times." But perhaps He might have been thinking to Himself, "The day will really come when Peter will die for Me." As they entered the garden, the Lord said to His disciples, "Pray with me so that you might worthily pass through the coming temptation." In the garden, the Savior went off by Himself and began to ask His Heavenly Father, "If it be Your will, let this Cup pass from Me but nevertheless, not My will but Yours be done." When He went back to His disciples, He saw that they were not praying but sleeping.

When he opened his eyes, before he had fully woken up, Peter saw strange lights between the dark trees and a gray figure approaching the Savior. It was Judas. He came up to Christ and greeted Him and kissed Him, giving a sign to the guards who were with him. They were supposed to seize the One Whom the traitor kissed. The guards didn't know who to arrest because they didn't even know what Christ looked like, which explains a lot. Usually, the people who make war against Christ don't really know Him. They don't know what He is really like and that is why they fight against Him.

HOT AND COLD

Christ had been arrested. Just as He had foretold, most of the Apostles had fled in fear but Peter had decided not to abandon his Teacher no matter what. He followed Christ at a safe distance. The prisoner was taken to the house of the chief priest to face judgment. While Christ was waiting in the courtyard to be judged, Peter sat at a campfire not far away. The night was very cold. "Who are you?" someone nearby asked Peter. "Didn't you come with Him?" the curious person asked, pointing at Christ. "Who me? No..." Peter muttered and stopped looking in Christ's direction.

"Of course you are! I can see right away that you're not from

Jerusalem. That means you must be one of them," the man insisted, not backing down. "No, my good man, you're mistaken. I'm here... because my mother-in-law is sick," the Apostle said, trying to justify himself. Unfortunately for him, at this point a nearby woman joined in the conversation: "Why are you lying? I saw you with Him myself!" "I do not know that Man!" Peter cried out, jumping to his feet. The Bible mentions one detail in passing but what a detail it is! At that moment when Peter denied Him for the third time, Christ looked at Peter and the Apostle's very soul grew cold. He had lied because he just wanted to warm himself at the fire and wanted to be left alone. But while our bodies might feel warm when we're near a fire, our souls are only truly warm when we're near God. When we are not faithful to God, our souls grow cold.

THE CROSS

When the result is known in advance, a trial goes very quickly. Christ was sentenced to a shameful death by crucifixion. Along with two thieves, He was nailed to a cross. "By His wounds we have all been healed," Isaiah had prophesied. Yes, the voluntary sacrificial death of the Lamb of God brought us the deliverance from sin. Christ gave us the medicine we needed for the horrible disease of sin. He gave us Himself, His own Body and Blood. On the Cross, the Lord gave salvation to all of us. But during those last few hours of His earthly life, He showed special concern for two people. He gave His Mother, Mary, into the care of the Apostle John and He also helped one of the thieves who were crucified with Him to repent and to cleanse his soul of all sin. We often tell ourselves that we can't help others because "our hands are tied." But Christ's hands were nailed to the Cross and He still cared for others until His last breath.

THE GRAVE

Once, Christ had said, "In order for a seed to grow and bear fruit, it must first die and be buried in the Earth." The Savior Himself became that seed when He died and was buried in order to rise from the dead and bring us all joy. In order to get to that moment, the Savior's disciples had to live through the worst days of their lives. They took His body and prepared it for burial. They hurried because the Sabbath was coming when, as the Jews believed, it was forbidden to do any work at all.

However, Christ Himself explained to His disciples that this commandment was misunderstood. The Sabbath wasn't a day for laziness. On the contrary, on the Sabbath we should work even harder for God's glory by doing good, God-pleasing works. But the disciples weren't thinking about that now. They now had to talk about their Teacher in the past tense and they couldn't wrap their minds around that. Besides these sad thoughts, they also had many questions floating around their heads. "What will become of us now?" "Was the Teacher not really the promised Savior?" and many others...

CHRIST IS RISEN!

However, they had no time to look for answers to these questions. The Sabbath wasn't even hours, but rather just minutes, away. Getting a hold of themselves, they said, "We'll have to think about all of that tomorrow. Right now, we must perform our last duty for our Teacher." Because of their hurry, they didn't have time to anoint his body with all the burial spices and so some women who had served the Savior agreed to come back to His tomb the morning after the Sabbath to perform the burial rites. The Sabbath passed (the longest and most dreadful Sabbath in their lives) and the sun had not yet risen when the women disciples of the Lord hurried to the tomb of the Teacher. They had cried so much that their tears had run dry. Only one thing was worrying them: who would roll away the heavy stone from the door of the tomb? However, when they got to the tomb, a different question arose – what had happened?! The tomb was opened and the burial clothes were glistening in the darkness. The Body of Christ had disappeared! The women probably thought of all sorts of dreadful explanations for what they saw but at that moment, an Angel appeared to them and said, "Why do you seek the Living among the dead? He is not here. He is risen!" Still unable fully to believe what they heard, the women rushed home and on the way, Christ Himself appeared to them, alive and well!

A HEART ON FIRE

What had just happened was unbelievable! Although, why was it so unbelievable? Everything that the Apostles knew about Christ should have convinced them that it had to be this way. The Savior had raised the dead many times before their very eyes and only a week before had done something even more incredible: He had raised Lazarus who had been dead for four days. Besides, on multiple occasions, the Lord had told His disciples that He would rise from the dead soon after his death. But they still had doubts. The day that Christ rose from the dead (which is why ever since, Sunday has been called "the day of Resurrection"), two of His disciples were heading to a nearby city on business. A stranger joined them and began to ask them why they were so sad. When they told him what was going on, he was surprised and said, "But that is how it should be! The Savior had to die and then rise from the dead. That is what all the prophets taught." Afterwards, the stranger began to mention Biblical prophecies about the Christ and then... suddenly disappeared! "I see!" one of the disciples cried out. "What?" the other asked. "Personally, I'm very confused." "That was Christ Himself! That is why the whole way my heart burned within me when I was near Him." "Yes, yes!" the other said, "I felt the same thing!"

PEACE BE TO YOU

That very same day, the risen Lord appeared to His closest disciples. The first thing that He said to them was: "Peace be to you!" Christians are often reproached for talking too much about something called "humility." What exactly is "humility"? It doesn't

mean that you need to agree with everything people say or let them wipe their feet on you. Humility is connected with peacefulness. It is when we preserve spiritual peace. Christ not only called us to peace with His words but He gave us an example of what it is to love peace. So when one of His disciples said that he wouldn't believe in Christ's resurrection unless he touched His wounds himself, Christ reacted peacefully. He told him to put out his hand and touch. Christ also made peace with Peter. The fact that He made peace with Peter doesn't mean that before that, He was upset with him. Christ's soul was always peaceful. Peter's soul, however, was in turmoil. After he talked to the Savior, though, the grace of peace returned to Peter. The Lord spent forty days with His disciples and then ascended into His Heavenly Kingdom.

THE COMFORTER

Before His Ascension, Christ promised that He wouldn't leave His disciples and those who would believe in Him through their words, without help. At the Passover, Christ gave the disciples the first Communion. Then, on the fiftieth day after His Resurrection, the Lord sent them the Comforter, the Holy Spirit. On that day, they gathered together in Jerusalem and suddenly, there was a noise like thunder coming from the clear sky. Afterwards, a tongue of fire descended on each of the Apostles and then things got even more interesting. Each of them began to praise God in languages that they hadn't known before. Through this miracle, the Lord showed the disciples that each of them would be sent to preach about Him to distant lands.

Of course, the Holy Spirit did more than just give the Apostles the ability to speak different languages. The Holy Spirit taught them to speak in the language of the human heart. Immediately after this, Peter went outside and began to preach Christ, and his words were so convincing that three thousand people believed and were baptized that very day. That is how the Church was born. In Holy Baptism, each Christian receives the gift of the Holy Spirit. What does the Holy Spirit give those whom He abides in? Christ said that everything should be judged by its fruits. The Apostle Paul told us what the fruits of the Spirit are. The Holy Spirit instills in us love, joy, peace, long-suffering, goodness, mercy, faith, meekness, and self-control.

THE LAST SHALL BE FIRST

The Apostle Paul wasn't originally one of Christ's twelve closest disciples. Nevertheless, he became the most renowned and honored of the Apostles. The story of Paul is a marvelous example of how Christ can turn even His sworn enemies into dear friends. At first, Paul was a zealous Pharisee who cruelly persecuted Christians. Once, he went with an armed detachment to the city of Damascus to arrest the Christians there. On the road, he was blinded by a bright light and he heard a voice from Heaven, "Why do you persecute Me?" "Who are you?" Paul asked. "I am Jesus Whom you are persecuting" he heard in response. At that moment, Paul was temporarily blinded physically, but spiritually began to see.

The name Paul (like the name Peter) was given to the Apostle by Christ Himself. "Paul" means "little one" but it isn't an insult since, according to Christ, the one who would be first must become last of all and the one who would be great must first become small like a child. Paul became the greatest of the Apostles, preaching Christ throughout almost the whole Roman Empire. He was small but bold. His great accomplishment was that he was the first to understand that Christ came not only to save the chosen Jewish people but all people. All of them! And that meant that Christ should be preached to all nations. That message came to be called "the Gospel" which means "good news."

And no news could be better than that!

FAITHFUL WITNESSES

In the Gospel it says: "Seek first the Kingdom of God and His righteousness and everything else shall be added to you." The Lord calls those who dedicate their lives to the search for righteousness "blessed," or "happy." He says, "Blessed are those who hunger and thirst after righteousness for they shall be filled with it." When he talks about "thirsting after righteousness," the Lord is showing us that God's righteousness is like water which we cannot live without. He also warns us, though, that for the sake of righteousness we will be reproached, hated, and persecuted.

People are afraid of truth and righteousness because they are not only like water but also like light and they illumine everything that is dark and hidden, everything that lurks in the shadows, the things that we are afraid to admit even to ourselves. It often seems like it is easier to live without truth and righteousness but that isn't really true. It's true that if you live in the darkness, you don't need to clean up after yourself, to dust and vacuum, but is it really better to live in filth rather than in cleanliness? Christians are those who choose cleanliness over filth. However, that choice often contains a hidden danger. For the first three centuries, Christians were severely persecuted. They were arrested, interrogated, sent into exile, tortured and killed. These Christians were called "martyrs" which in Greek means "witnesses," because they bore witness to the world about God's righteousness. Often, when Christians were executed, it was a public spectacle. They were led out into the arena (even women, children, and the elderly) and then hungry lions were let loose. During the last minutes of their earthly lives, the martyrs prayed but no one except the One they prayed to heard what they said because the area was filled with the roaring of the hungry beasts and the cries of the bloodthirsty crowd. Of course, we can't help but feel sorry for them... Not for the martyrs (everything turned out well for them) but for the crowd whose souls were so darkened and hardened that they found pleasure in the sight of the sufferings of others. Because of their spiritual blindness, they missed out on the most important part of the spectacle, when Angels came and took the souls of the martyrs to their heavenly abodes.

PRINCE VLADIMIR'S SECRET

Remember that Christ said that if a seed dies, it will be reborn and bring forth abundant fruit. That was what happened with the Christian martyrs. Christ preached for three years in Israel and on the day of the Holy Spirit's descent, the Church already numbered three thousand people. Afterwards, Christians were cruelly persecuted for three centuries but new Christians took the place of those who were executed. Sometimes, people decided to become Christians when they saw how the martyrs bravely endured their sufferings for the sake of God's righteousness. But what drew people even more wasn't the firmness the Christians showed but rather their gentleness, the zeal they showed in loving their neighbors. Christ Himself spoke about this: "Let your light so shine before men that they may see your good works and glorify your Father who is in Heaven." At the beginning of the 4th century, Emperor Constantine the Great put an end to the persecutions and Christians were allowed to preach the Gospel freely. The Church began to spread quickly beyond the bounds of the Roman Empire. Around the 9th century, thanks to the labors of two brothers, Saints Kyrill and Methodius, Christianity even reached a land called Rus. In 988, their prince, Prince Vladimir, baptized his people. However, before transforming his country, he first had to transform himself. Thanks to his new faith, he went from being a cruel and dishonest man to being a humble and merciful father, beloved by his people.

Historians like to try to guess what the secret was as to why

Christianity spread so quickly throughout Vladimir's lands. The true secret was revealed by St. Seraphim of Sarov when he said, "Acquire the Spirit of Peace and thousands around you will be saved." A large part of the success of the preaching of the Gospel in this new land depended on the holy Prince Vladimir himself. Thousands of hearts were set alight for God by his heart, which burned with the love of God.

THE END AND A NEW BEGINNING

Sometimes, when Christian hearts start to grow cold, they become like the Pharisees from the Gospels. While they may be Christians on the outside, rather than having the Kingdom of God in their hearts, the Evil One reigns. So God, in order to rekindle the flame in their hearts, allows a strong wind of persecution to blow. That is what happened in Russia when a revolution came.

Hardship reveals what is most important to us. Before the Revolution, people could live in a gray area, between God and the Devil, but the Revolution forced them to choose whose side they were on. Brother betrayed brother and children betrayed their parents. The blood of the martyrs once again flowed freely. The Church went through the worst period of persecution and yet, at the same time, an amazing spiritual rebirth.

TODAY

Today, we live in a time of peace where the horrible persecutions of the 20th century have faded (although not everywhere in the world). Will this time of peace be a time of renewal, when Christianity will flower like it did in the 4th century? The only way to answer that question clearly is with the word "if." Yes, if we become true Christians, if when people look at us, they wonder how we were able to become so happy, peaceful, compassionate, brave, noble, and honorable; if they wonder what our secret is, and how to become like us, then it will be.

But there is no secret. The "recipe" for making a true Christian out of an ordinary person is easy to find on the pages of the Gospels. Many people mistakenly think that in order to become a true Christian, a citizen of the Kingdom of Heaven, we need to stop being human and become some sort of heavenly being, an Angel. But that isn't true. Our souls are already created to be Christian. God created us according to His "image and likeness," and made us human beings. Our task is to preserve our true humanity, which is created in His image. This means preserving goodness, honesty, and purity of heart. We need to go through life by the straight paths, avoiding lying and deceit. If we fall and stain our souls, we must pick ourselves back up and shake off the dirt. In other words, we should repent and fix our mistake and then boldly continue our journey. Christ is the way, the truth, and the Life. That means that He isn't only the goal but the path that leads to the goal. The Lord doesn't only meet us at the end of our path through life but He Himself leads us along that path. We need only to trust Him. He is always near.

Even right this very minute.

THE HERO OF OUR TIME
(Epilogue)

That is all that I wanted to say to you but it isn't the end because Sacred History isn't over. It began many years ago with the creation of the world and the first man, Adam, and continues today, with you. That is why this book is called "Sacred History from Adam to Me." It is your job to write a chapter for tomorrow, a chapter that you will write with your own words and actions, through the choices you make each day, each day that God gives you.

www.ingramcontent.com/pod-product-compliance
Lightning Source LLC
Chambersburg PA
CBHW051348110526
44591CB00025B/2940